MELBOURN

THE CITY AT A GLANC

C000228132

Southern Cross Station
The undulating, wave-like roof
obvious aspect of the £280m r
of Spencer Street Station, whicl
in time for the 2006 Commonwealth Games.
See p068

Docklands
This once industrial zone is now a thriving
area with apartments, restaurants, a public art
walk, parks and the Telstra Dome stadium
(740 Bourke Street, T 8625 7700).

Rialto Towers
These twin steel and glass office blocks are the
highest in the southern hemisphere. There's a
great view from the Level 55 observation deck.
525 Collins Street, T 9614 5888

Federation Square
This controversial development combines
ground-breaking architecture with arts and
leisure facilities on the banks of the Yarra.
See p014

Kings Domain
A 106-acre series of parks by the river that
surrounds Government House, the Shrine
of Remembrance, the Sidney Myer Music Bowl
and runs into the Royal Botanic Gardens.

Eureka Tower
Designed by Fender Katsalidis Architects, this
'vertical city' has 91 floors and, at 297m, is one
of the tallest residential buildings in the world.
See p009

Crown Entertainment Complex
This fun palace boasts two hotels (see p030),
a casino, restaurants, nightclubs, theatres,
bars, cinemas and a bowling alley.
8 Whiteman Street, T 9292 8888

INTRODUCTION
THE CHANGING FACE OF THE URBAN SCENE

This is a city for urban explorers. Much of what Melbourne has to offer to visitors – and that includes everything from architecture and art to shopping and culinary excellence – is hidden. It's not that Melburnians want to keep secret the gems they enjoy from day to day; it's just that the evolution of the city around a grid pattern has meant the lanes running off the main thoroughfares offer a more economical means for creative entrepreneurs to base businesses in the thick of it. In the past 20 years, with help from local government, these lanes have flourished. It's a fascinating layer that, to the uninitiated – and those who only look up towards the skyscrapers – could be virtually undetectable.

Beyond the centre of Melbourne, the inner-city suburbs have a village atmosphere. You should explore eclectic, bohemian Fitzroy, chichi, upmarket South Yarra and the laid-back bayside enclave of St Kilda for an insight into the city's multiple personalities.

Melbourne has a vibrant cultural life, witnessed not just in its myriad arts venues but in the structures that house them. The city's built history has been well preserved and some of its local architects, such as Denton Corker Marshall and Sean Godsell, are internationally acclaimed. In this town, a bar is not just a place to drink, but also a venue for artists to present their work and for designers to create unique spaces. As for the food…this is one of the best places to eat out in the world.

ESSENTIAL INFO
FACTS, FIGURES AND USEFUL ADDRESSES

TOURIST OFFICE
Melbourne Visitor Centre
Federation Square
Swanston Street/Flinders Street
T 9658 9658
www.thatsmelbourne.com.au

TRANSPORT
Car hire
Hertz
97 Franklin Street
T 9663 6244
Metlink
T 131 638
www.metlinkmelbourne.com.au
Taxi
Silver Top Taxi
T 131 008

EMERGENCY SERVICES
Emergencies
T 000
Late-night pharmacy (until midnight)
Tambassis Pharmacy
Sydney Road/Brunswick Road
T 9387 8830

CONSULATES
British Consulate-General
17th floor, 90 Collins Street
T 9652 1670
bhc.britaus.net
US Consulate-General
553 St Kilda Road
T 9526 5900
melbourne.usconsulate.gov

MONEY
American Express
233 Collins Street
T 1300 139 060
travel.americanexpress.com

POSTAL SERVICES
Post Office
250 Elizabeth Street
T 131 318
Shipping
UPS
100 William Street
T 9670 4488
www.ups.com

BOOKS
The Birth of Melbourne by Tim Flannery
(Text Publishing)
Monkey Grip by Helen Garner (Penguin)
My Brother Jack by George Johnston
(HarperCollins)
Three Dollars by Elliot Perlman
(Riverhead Trade)

WEBSITES
Art
www.ngv.vic.gov.au
www.accaonline.org.au
Design
www.nationaldesigncentre.com
www.craftvic.asn.au
Newspapers
www.theage.com.au
www.news.com.au

COST OF LIVING
**Taxi from Melbourne Airport
to city centre**
£30
Cappuccino
£1.25
Packet of cigarettes
£4.50
Daily newspaper
£0.50
Bottle of champagne
£40

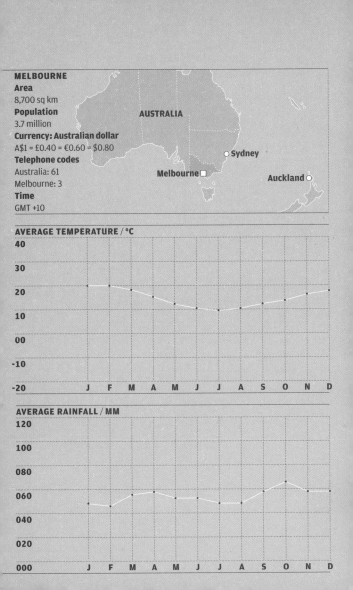

MELBOURNE
Area
8,700 sq km
Population
3.7 million
Currency: Australian dollar
A$1 = £0.40 = €0.60 = $0.80
Telephone codes
Australia: 61
Melbourne: 3
Time
GMT +10

AUSTRALIA

Sydney
Melbourne
Auckland

AVERAGE TEMPERATURE / °C

	J	F	M	A	M	J	J	A	S	O	N	D

40
30
20
00
-10
-20

AVERAGE RAINFALL / MM

120
100
080
060
040
020
000

| J | F | M | A | M | J | J | A | S | O | N | D |

NEIGHBOURHOODS

THE AREAS YOU NEED TO KNOW AND WHY

To help you navigate the city, we've chosen the most interesting districts (see below and the map inside the back cover) and colour-coded our featured venues, according to their location; those venues that are outside these areas are not coloured.

CENTRAL BUSINESS DISTRICT

The CBD is not only Melbourne's business heart but also harbours shopping, eating, drinking and arts haunts. Unlike similar areas in other cities, the CBD never sleeps. If you're on a tight schedule, you can find everything you need here, although it would be a shame not to venture further. Melbourne's famous trams run all over the city and are one of the easiest ways to get from one end of town to the other.

SOUTHBANK

It might be just across the river from the CBD but Southbank has a totally different feel to it. Very densely developed, it is home to the massive Crown Complex, which includes the Crown Towers hotel (see p030), the Rockpool Bar & Grill (see p048) and the Arts Centre (100 St Kilda Road, T 9281 8000), with its Sunday crafts market. Tourists and locals alike come here to enjoy the river views.

CARLTON

When Italian migrants flocked to the city after WWII, most settled around Carlton, so there's no such thing as a bad espresso here. There are also great shops, including Readings Books (309 Lygon Street, T 9347 6633), cinemas and, of course, excellent restaurants along Lygon Street. If you find it hard to resist Italian pastries, walk round the corner to Brunetti (194-204 Faraday Street, T 9347 2801) for one of the most tempting selections in the city.

ST KILDA

For sun and sand, head to this popular bayside suburb – the setting for Australian TV series *The Secret Life of Us*. There are two halves to this district: rowdy, rough-and-ready Fitzroy Street and the more genteel Acland Street, with its bookstores and fancy cake shops. On the waterfront are the pier, St Kilda Sea Baths (part of the South Pacific Health Club, see p089) and Luna Park (Lower Esplanade, T 9525 5033).

SOUTH YARRA

Parts of this neighbourhood feel like a quaint and exclusive village. It is bordered on two sides by the Royal Botanic Gardens and Fawkner Park, so it's also rather green and leafy. High-end shopping can be found along Toorak Road and Chapel Street, and the restaurants in this area are among the best in Melbourne. Base yourself at the intimate Lyall Hotel (see p016) to explore all that this fascinating suburb has to offer.

FITZROY

This arty, bohemian enclave has really come alive in the past 10 years – until recently the trendy Builder's Arms Hotel (211 Gertrude Street, T 9419 0818) was the favoured haunt of local gangsters. The main thoroughfare, Brunswick Street, has so many cafés and shops, you won't know where to start. Venture down Johnston Street to find the city's Spanish community, and the clubs, restaurants and flamenco bars that go with it.

LANDMARKS

THE SHAPE OF THE CITY SKYLINE

Melbourne has been blessed with the patronage of great aesthetes since the first European settlers arrived in 1835. Grand mansions from that era survive, while trams and cars still travel along wide, tree-lined promenades. In more recent years, some of Australia's finest architects have made their mark on what would otherwise have been a very flat, rather ugly city landscape.

Since the mid- to late 1990s, Melbourne has seen extensive redevelopment and expansion of its major cultural venues, as well as something of an upward trajectory. Italian architect and designer Mario Bellini oversaw a 2003 overhaul of the National Gallery of Victoria International (180 St Kilda Road, T 8620 2222), while the 297m Eureka Tower (7 Riverside Quay, www.eurekatower.com.au) by Fender Katsalidis Architects opened in October 2006, with a public observation deck on Level 88. An eye has also been kept on the past, and important older buildings, such as Como Historic House (Williams Road/Lechlade Avenue, T 9827 2500), which dates back to 1847 and is now part of the National Trust of Australia's portfolio, have been restored and preserved.

Interestingly, though, some of the city's most readily identified landmarks, such as the MCG (see p012), are the product of one of its major obsessions – sport. And to gloss over them would be to ignore Melbourne's beating heart.

For full addresses, see Resources.

Melbourne Gateway

Denton Corker Marshall's urban sculpture welcomes visitors to the city on the way in from Tullamarine Airport. Fans of this Melbourne architectural firm will recognise its signature marks — bright colours and abstract shapes — all over the project. Thirty-nine angled red beams on the right-hand side of the road form a guard of honour, while a 70m yellow beam (local wags refer to it as the 'Cheesestick') is cantilevered across the highway from the opposite side of the road. There's also a metal sound tube that protects nearby housing from freeway noise. According to the architects: 'The yellow beam acts as a symbolic archway — the urban equivalent of a boom gate in the up position. The result is a powerful and dynamic gesture that opens up the city to visitors.'
Tullamarine Freeway

MCG

Sport is a religion in this city and the Melbourne Cricket Ground (MCG) is the main place of worship; devotees flock to watch cricket in the summer and Aussie Rules (AFL) in winter. The Melbourne Cricket Club took over this central site in 1853 and the first grandstand was built a year later. The latest redevelopment, by Jackson Architecture, was completed in 2006 and means that the ground can now hold 100,000 spectators – and it's standing room only during big events, such as the AFL grand final held on the last Saturday in September. On non-event days, take a tour or visit the brand-new National Sports Museum – an attraction that's long overdue for a country with such an outstanding sporting tradition.
Yarra Park, Brunton Avenue, T 9657 8867, www.mcg.org.au

Republic Tower

One of the biggest successes of the 1990s building boom, which was a direct result of the then Liberal premier Jeff Kennett's privatisation programme, was this roundly praised residential building designed by Fender Katsalidis Architects. All sculptural concrete fins and dark glass, it consists of 36 storeys of apartments atop a five-level mixed-use podium. One of its most interesting aspects is the huge billboard, overseen by the Visible Art Foundation, which changes its display regularly. Artists whose work has been featured include Guo Jian and Patricia Piccinini.

Queen Street/La Trobe Street

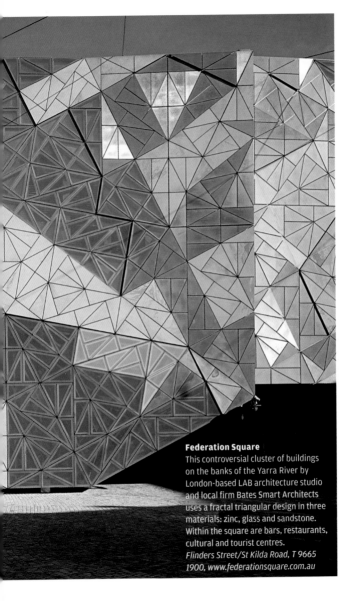

Federation Square
This controversial cluster of buildings on the banks of the Yarra River by London-based LAB architecture studio and local firm Bates Smart Architects uses a fractal triangular design in three materials: zinc, glass and sandstone. Within the square are bars, restaurants, cultural and tourist centres.
Flinders Street/St Kilda Road, T 9665 1900, www.federationsquare.com.au

HOTELS
WHERE TO STAY AND WHICH ROOMS TO BOOK

Like almost every other big city in the world, Melbourne offers visitors a good range of big-name hotels. The Sofitel (25 Collins Street, T 9653 0000) is very comfortable and is set in a great location – what locals refer to as the 'Paris' end of Collins Street, due to its leafy aspect and luxury stores – while the plush Park Hyatt (1 Parliament Square, T 9224 1234) is also popular.

This being a city proud of its design heritage, it should come as no surprise that there is a fine selection of boutique dwellings. The Adelphi (see p022), which opened in 1993 and underwent floor-by-floor renovations in 2007, is one of Australia's hippest hotels, and the makeover has ensured that it'll retain those credentials for many years to come. On a residential street in South Yarra is the sophisticated Lyall Hotel (14 Murphy Street, T 9868 8222), a favoured destination for visiting magazine editors and the fashion pack; we like Suite 401, which has two balconies. In the same area, you'll find exquisite service at The Hatton (see p023) and every facility you could wish for at The Como (opposite). If you want to be close to the beach, then head to St Kilda and the much-loved and very chichi The Prince (see p020).

Hotels in Melbourne usually fill up fast during major sporting events, such as the Australian Open tennis tournament in January and the Grand Prix in mid-March, so book well in advance.
For full addresses and room rates, see Resources.

The Como

Situated on the corner of Toorak Road and Chapel Street, both of which are lined with shops, bars and cafés, this is a great spot to experience a lot without moving too far. The hotel has 107 rooms and suites, such as the Open-Plan Suite (above). We recommend splashing out on a Spa Suite, which boasts a bathtub for two. There are various configurations at the Como, however, and some suites come with an office area, a fully equipped kitchen and even a Japanese garden on a private balcony. On a hot sunny day, the rooftop pool (overleaf) is the place to be. *630 Chapel Street, T 9825 2222, www.mirvachotels.com*

Rooftop pool, The Como

The Prince

This art deco building has been at the heart of St Kilda life for decades, and John and Frank van Haandel recognised this when they converted it into a series of businesses during the 1990s. Here you will find the Mink vodka bar (T 9536 1199), Circa restaurant (T 9536 1122), Il Fornaio bakery (T 9534 2922), Aurora Spa Retreat (see p088) and this boutique hotel. Mixing urban chic with beachside cool, The Prince is always heavily booked, despite some of the 40 rooms being on the small side. We recommend Room 413 (above) on the top floor, for its views over St Kilda and the ocean, and the huge tub in the bathroom.
2 Acland Street, T 9536 1111,
www.theprince.com.au

Adelphi

When it opened in the early 1990s, in an old warehouse reconfigured by architects Denton Corker Marshall, the Adelphi – all bright colours and sharp lines – quickly became the hotel of choice for designers and creatives. The recent overhaul by Smart Design Studio, overseen by DCM, gave the hotel's 34 rooms a softer, more comfortable feel and a bar was added to the ground floor. The famous rooftop pool (above), which is made of Perspex and cantilevered over the street, remains. Its deck is just the place to spend a sunny, late Melbourne afternoon. In the hotel basement is the excellent restaurant, Ezard (T 9639 6811).
187 Flinders Lane, T 9650 7555, www.adelphi.com.au

The Hatton

It's all about service at this boutique hotel, which features 20 simply designed rooms housed in an Italianate building. Guests keep coming back for the comfort, the friendly faces and the location, on a tram stop and near the Botanical Gardens. The rooftop terrace, where you can breakfast in the sun, is a great place to watch the New Year's Eve fireworks. The colourful reception area doubles as a café and bar.

Opt for the Eastern Balcony Suite (above), with its Japanese influences, verandah and freestanding bath. Alternatively, a Superior Room (overleaf) or Courtyard Superior Room on the ground floor are both good options. Dine at the nearby Botanical (T 9820 7888), where chef Paul Wilson serves up delicious steaks. *65 Park Street, T 9868 4800, www.hatton.com.au*

Superior Room, The Hatton

The Marque Hotel

Get close to the beach at this suitably relaxed 80-room hotel. Everything is bright and airy in the bedrooms, such as the Executive Room (above), and there are Bulgari products in the bathrooms. The Play Room, a round suite with a spa bath at the foot of the bed, will either appeal to your sense of fun or leave you completely bemused. The Marque is located in a bustling part of St Kilda, not quite as smart as nearby Acland Street, so you'll find plenty of life here. Downstairs is Suger (T 8530 8888), which does a great breakfast, but for dinner head across the street to Mirka at the Tolarno Hotel (T 9525 3088), Italian chef Guy Grossi's latest restaurant. Light sleepers should know that the street can be noisy, especially at the weekend, so ask for a room at the back of the hotel.

35-37 Fitzroy Street, T 8530 8888,
www.rendezvoushotels.com

Hotel Lindrum

Architects Swaney Draper have created one of those sophisticated boutique hotels you wish you could live in, and Terry Fripp and Neil Bradford's rich-toned furnishings ensure that it's a wonderfully calming retreat after a hectic day or night. The Deluxe Rooms (above) overlook the MCG (see p012) and Botanical Gardens, while from the larger Junior Suites you can peer into the laneways (see p039). This grand building has had many incarnations, and was formerly owned by the Lindrums, a famous snooker-playing family. The theme has been carried subtly throughout the hotel and you can play a game on an original table in the bar.
26 Flinders Street, T 9668 1111,
www.hotellindrum.com.au

Crown Towers
This five-star, 482-room property, part of a complex that includes the city's casino, is lavish. Ask for a Deluxe Suite, on the corner of the building, or book into a Crystal Club Villa (pictured) – it comes with a private lift and eye-popping views. The pool and gym at the Crown Spa (T 9292 6182) are also a cut above. *8 Whiteman Street, T 9292 6868, www.crowntowers.com.au*

24 HOURS
SEE THE BEST OF THE CITY IN JUST ONE DAY

Melbourne delivers on three of the most important aspects of a city destination – great food, excellent shopping and cultural experiences unlike those you'll have anywhere else. And it is possible to enjoy all of these in one day – if you absolutely must. The trick is to use the excellent tram system that criss-crosses the city and its inner suburbs (the 112 travels to Brunswick Street; the 86 from Gertrude Street back to the centre). Luckily, you'll never have to worry about where to get your caffeine fix, as it's unlikely you'll ever be served a less-than-perfect espresso in this town.

Have your first cup of coffee at Melbourne institution Mario's (opposite), where breakfast is served all day. Then walk to the Centre for Contemporary Photography (404 George Street, T 9417 1549), which has four galleries designed by architect Sean Godsell. The shops of Gertrude Street (see p034) should be your next stop and the local *enoteca* (see p035) for lunch. Post *panino*, head to Flinders Lane (see p036), where you can view one of the city's excellent public art projects in Centre Place. Just minutes away from here is Riverland (Vaults 1-9, Federation Wharf, T 9662 1771), the ideal spot for a sunset drink. Make a reservation at Taxi Dining Room (see p038) for dinner with a view, and remember that in Melbourne the night never ends with dessert. The laneways (see p039) – an entire city of tiny bars – await you. *For full addresses, see Resources.*

09.00 Mario's

Don't be surprised if you have to wait a while for a table here. This is the most popular breakfast spot in Fitzroy – and with good reason. Mario's was opened in the mid-1980s by the two eponymous owners, when they decided to expand their successful catering company, so they've had plenty of time to get it right. Crisp tablecloths and waistcoated waiters belie the pleasantly grungy atmosphere of this neighbourhood hangout. The eggs Benedict and excellent coffee will be more than sufficient to gird you for the day. *303 Brunswick Street, T 9417 3343*

11.00 Gertrude Street

Over the past few years, this street has transformed itself from raggedy shopping strip into slick retail thoroughfare. Head to Shop Sui (T 9415 9588) for its eclectic mix of fashion, jewellery and knick-knacks; Books for Cooks (T 8415 1415); Industria (T 9417 1117) for its quirky collectables; Obüs (T 9416 0012) for designer dresses; Spacecraft for hand-printed fabrics and linens (T 9486 0010); and Amor y Locura (T 9486 0270) for architectural artefacts. Around the corner is Tongue and Groove (above; T 9416 0349), which has three levels filled with vintage and contemporary furniture and accessories. If you can't fit one of David Trubridge's 'Sling Recliners' into your suitcase, there are plenty more items that you will be able to pack, such as ceramics by Greg Bonasera and David Eliot and lighting by Marc Pascal.

13.00 The Gertrude Street Enoteca

This fine *enoteca*, owned by popular Melbourne chef Brigitte Hafner and her partner James Broadway (a player in the Slow Food movement in Australia), has a wall of wine and exquisite delicatessen products on display. On the lunchtime menu you'll find *panini*, homemade tarts, salads and an antipasti plate that people can't stop raving about. To accompany the food, as is to be expected in an *enoteca*, you can choose from an impressive selection of wines, which here draws on the Old and New Worlds.

229 Gertrude Street, T 9415 8262,
www.gertrudestreetenoteca.com

15.00 Flinders Lane
This long street has galleries, shops and great cafés. At the eastern end, there's Craft Victoria (T 9650 7775), which shows works by artists such as Susan Cohn (*I Protest: Love No War (3)*, pictured left) and has an excellent store. Also visit the Anna Schwartz Gallery (T 9654 6131) and Bobby's Cuts (T 9663 4030), a menswear outlet decked out like a butcher's shop.

19.30 Taxi Dining Room

Everything about this restaurant indicates that dinner here is going to be a memorable experience. Located in Federation Square (see p014), its night views of the glistening Southbank are stunning. Perch on the banquettes in the high-ceilinged dining room to peruse executive chef Michael Lambie's menu of global fusion dishes with a Japanese slant. For a starter, we highly recommend the Wagyu beef tataki with hot and sour dressing. Main courses include the delicious roast breast and confit of organic duck with celeriac purée and ginger orange jus, or let Lambie create a degustation menu for you.

Level 1, Transport Hotel, Federation Square, T 9654 8808, www.transporthotel.com.au

23.00 The laneways

Don't call it a night just yet. If you don't wander the laneways late in the evening, you'll miss out on the real Melbourne. Want to sip Indonesian Bintang beer and listen to cool tunes? Then head for Section 8 (27-29 Tattersalls Lane), a bar constructed from shipping containers, where the seats are piled-up pallets. Prefer some art and cocktails? Loop (T 9654 0500) offers up installations with experimental music and films. The Croft Institute (above; T 9671 4399) is a bizarre but brilliant mix of interior themes, from lab to hospital waiting room to 1930s gym, spread over three floors. Still going at 3am? Go to the rocking Cherry (T 9639 8122), where the crowd likes to party.

URBAN LIFE

CAFÉS, RESTAURANTS, BARS AND NIGHTCLUBS

Ask a Melburnian to nominate their favourite line-up for a night out and you'll be bombarded with ideas. You could easily spend a fortune dining at a top restaurant – the 12-course tasting menu at Vue de Monde (overleaf) costs £105 without wine – then have martinis at Gin Palace (10 Russell Place, T 9654 0533), before going dancing at a wealth of late-night venues, such as Prahran's Boutique (134 Greville Street, T 9525 2322). Or you could trawl the local strips (Smith Street between Fitzroy and Collingwood, for example) and sample what the neighbourhood has to offer – great ethnic eateries, quirky pubs and bars that push on until daybreak.

The laneways offer up lots of gems, such as Hell's Kitchen (20a Centre Place, T 9654 5755), with its indie rock vibe, the laboratory-inspired Croft Institute (see p039) and that perennial favourite for wine-loving lounge lizards, the Melbourne Supper Club (Level 1, 161 Spring Street, T 9654 6300). In many of the smaller, local restaurants, you can bring your own wine – ask for the nearest bottle shop (local lingo for off-licence).

Melbourne's live music scene is also thriving, with venues that range from huge stadiums to tiny pubs. Try the Corner Hotel (57 Swan Street, T 9427 9198) in Richmond for beer-soaked rock or catch local and international stars at the Prince Bandroom (29 Fitzroy Street, T 9536 1168). Check listings in *The Age* on Fridays. *For full addresses, see Resources.*

Cookie

It's big, it's loud and it's a lot of fun – the perfect place to eat and drink at almost any time of day. Cookie's fiery Thai food is outrageously good and has acquired some very high-profile fans, including chef and author Anthony Bourdain. The huge room is dominated by the crazily decorated bar, where guys in suits mix with students and groovers. The music is cool, though it can be hard to hear over the crowd. Take a special companion late in the afternoon, snare one of the tables on the tiny balconies and stay the course. *1st floor, 252 Swanston Street, T 9663 7660, www.cookie.net.au*

Vue de Monde

Culinary wunderkind Shannon Bennett's elegant fine-diner in the CBD has won more awards than you can poke an egg whisk at. Every detail is attended to, right down to the handmade plates by Tasmanian artist Tom Samek, and the French food is prepared using the finest local ingredients. Think bistro classics updated and modernised, such as *agneau braisé* (slow-cooked lamb belly in a spicy curried tomato sauce with mint jelly). Tasting menus are created for each table; choose between five and 12 courses. Book the Chef's Table, located in the kitchen, for an unforgettable culinary experience. Bennett has also opened a bistro (Bistro Vue, T 9691 3838) and café (Café Vue, T 9691 3888) on the site.

Normanby Chambers Building,
430 Little Collins Street, T 9691 3888,
www.vuedemonde.com.au

MoVida

Spanish-born, Melbourne-raised Frank Camorra serves up exceptional food at his tiny tapas and wine bar. It's not unusual to see other chefs here on their days off, tucking into the modern interpretations of tapas at the high tables near the bar (there are main courses as well, but by ordering smaller dishes you can try so much more). There's also a conventional dining area if you prefer. We recommend you try the rabbit meatballs braised with calamari and lemon myrtle or scallops with *jamón* and potato foam. *1 Hosier Lane, T 9663 3038, www.movida.com.au*

Pearl Restaurant + Bar

There is something that's quintessentially Melbourne about Pearl. It's a beautiful, low-key room and bar that somehow feels special. Chef Geoff Lindsay's mod-Oz food incorporates many cuisines, especially Asian, and the wine list is one of the best in the city. There are two dishes you must try: the signature roast red duck curry and the Turkish delight and rose-petal ice cream with glacé ginger, pomegranate seeds and Persian fairy floss. So successful is Lindsay's restaurant that he's expanded to Hong Kong, where he has opened Pearl on the Peak.
631-633 Church Street, T 9421 4599, www.pearlrestaurant.com.au

Piadina Slow Food

This café hidden down a side lane is a great spot for a delicious breakfast or lunch. Everything is made on the premises, including the eponymous *piadinas* (Italian flat bread), and the menu is displayed on brown butcher's paper. Think pancetta, fontina and fried green tomato omelettes for breakfast, and slow-cooked meals, like marmalade beef, for lunch. This is a real hot spot during the week, so be prepared to share one of the three booths or arrive early to claim one of the tables in the courtyard.
57 Lonsdale Street, T 9662 2277

Melbourne Wine Room

The exterior of St Kilda's grand George Hotel looks a little faded, but inside the Melbourne Wine Room is a treasure. You can eat in the noisy, beery bar out front or choose the calm, elegant rear dining room. Chef Karen Martini, who is well known in Australia for her weekly column in *Sunday Life* magazine, serves up a menu of simple, modern Italian dishes, such as the restaurant's famous carpaccio. As you'd expect, the wine list, which features an excellent international selection, is truly something to behold.
125 Fitzroy Street, T 9525 5599

Rockpool Bar & Grill
Unlike Neil Perry's Sydney Rockpool,
his Melbourne venture, part of the
Crown Casino, is big, bold and buzzy.
The emphasis is on steaks — team Wagyu
or dry-aged beef with a rich potato and
cabbage gratin — but the lighter seafood
dishes, like the sashimi-style Four Raw
Tastes of the Sea, are also excellent.
Crown Complex, T 8648 1900,
www.rockpoolmelbourne.com

New Gold Mountain

Push through the door under the number 21 on one of Melbourne's laneways, climb the stairs and you'll find a sophisticated oriental room with jade tones, low stools and Mao posters. Up another flight of stairs is a mini-labyrinth of sexy private rooms separated by red laser-cut panels. Chinese lanterns and fabric installations hang from the ceiling and red patterned wallpaper matches the banquettes. An eclectic mix of tracks plays softly, there's an extensive range of whiskies and vodkas, an innovative cocktail and sours list and a small menu of Asian snacks. This is the place for long, late-night conversations; it's licensed until 5am. The name is what Chinese immigrants called each new mine during the gold-rush era in the 1850s.
Level 1, 21 Liverpool Street, T 9650 8859, www.newgoldmountain.org

Madame Brussels
It's a garden party every day and night
at this popular bar named after the city's
first brothel mogul. The elevator spits
you out into a room that is carpeted
in Astroturf and decorated with wicker
outdoor furniture (often topped with
a sprawling nymphet). Cute staff are
dressed as if they're about to tee off.
The roof terrace, with its views of the
city, is a highlight, and on colder nights
you are given a blanket to cover your
knees. In summer, on Sunday afternoons,
there's a barbecue with a guest chef from
one of Melbourne's leading restaurants;
past chargrillers have included Vue de
Monde's Shannon Bennett, Longrain's
Martin Boetz and Three One Two's Andrew
McConnell. A reservation is essential, as
is ordering a jug of Pimms on arrival.
*Level 3, 59-63 Bourke Street, T 9662 2775,
www.madamebrussels.com*

Ffour

It wouldn't be Melbourne if you could find it easily, but persisting in tracking down this futuristic bar that parties hard as the night wears on is worth the effort. The industrial interior features a lot of bright pink and is apparently inspired by MC Escher, the Bauhaus and Russia's constructivist period. Ffour delivers in all areas, though, offering great cocktails and a good selection of wine and beer,

and music varies from trance to retro pop, depending on the night. Step out onto the balcony if you need a breath of fresh air.
Level 2, 322 Little Collins Street,
T 9650 4494, www.ffour.com.au

Gingerboy

When chef Teage Ezard was working as a consultant for Hong Kong's JIA Hotel, he became fascinated with street food and decided that his next restaurant would be a more relaxed affair, serving hawker-style dishes designed to share. The result is Gingerboy, a small space designed by Elenberg Fraser. Walls lined with black lacquered bamboo are studded with tiny lights, a tasselled red chandelier dominates the room and Philippe Starck's 'Louis Ghost' chairs star at the tables. The food is equally impressive. Try the chilli salt cuttlefish, pork dumplings with shrimp and mint relish or caramelised Wagyu ox cheeks with ground peanuts and chilli.

27-29 Crossley Street, T 9662 4200, www.gingerboy.com.au

Mr Tulk
There is nothing quiet about the State
Library café, which is named after the
first chief librarian. Located in a grand
room decorated with a mural, it serves
up sardines with salsa verde, pâté with
cornichons and crostini, coffee and cake.
Anglepoise lamps over a central bench
will take you right back to college.
*State Library of Victoria, 328 Swanston
Street, T 8660 5700*

Polly

You could become a little overwhelmed by the lengthy cocktail list here – there are more than 50 to choose from – so why not get one of the nattily attired barmen to choose for you? We're rather fond of the Damage Control: coriander, mint, ginger and lime muddled with organic vodka, lychee liqueur, limoncello and cranberry juice. The deep red room with its squashy sofas and paintings of naked ladies has rococo overtones. The seating's arranged so that you can usually find a spot to suit, whether there are two of you or 20.
401 Brunswick Street, T 9419 6539, www.pollybar.com.au

Eve

Florence Broadhurst's wallpapers (above and overleaf) feature prominently in this space created by local design firm 21-19. It's all extremely chic and the technology is spot on (that's a one-of-a-kind dancefloor you're grooving on). Saturdays are the most glamorous and attract a fashion crowd, who pose on the plush, themed seating areas. Order cocktails at the gorgeous backlit marble bar with its crystal dragon watching over the action. You can put yourself on the guestlist via the website.
Lower level, 334 City Road, T 9696 7388, www.evebar.com.au

Eve

INSIDER'S GUIDE

BARRIE BARTON, PUBLISHER AND PROMOTER

Barton's ezines (www.threethousand.com.au) provide a weekly snapshot of what's happening in Melbourne's subcultures. He also runs Rooftop Cinema (Level 6, Curtin House, 252 Swanston Street, T 9663 3596) above Cookie (see p041) in the summer, and likes to make the most of the fact that he lives and works in the centre of the city. For breakfast, he recommends going al fresco at City Wine Shop (159 Spring Street, T 9654 6657), which he describes as 'a tiny slice of Europe'. Barton's favourite place for dinner is Yu-u (137 Flinders Lane, T 9639 7073), a tiny Japanese restaurant with incredible food, staff who speak very little English, and no sign. 'Finding it is half the fun,' he says, 'but make sure you book.' Also recommended is the dark and brooding Il Bacaro (168-170 Little Collins Street, T 9654 6778), for its uncompromising Italian menu. 'It's all about the food here, but the atmosphere is great too.'

One of the things that Barton loves about Melbourne is that 'you can become part of a community that is forged on nothing more than drinking in the same café'. One of his favourites is Wall Two 80 (280 Carlisle Street, T 9593 8280) in Balaclava, basically a hole-in-the-wall with a communal table, designed by Six Degrees. And for drinks and mixing, he suggests Matt McConnell's casual tapas place Bar Lourinhã (37 Little Collins Street, T 9663 7890), which is continuously packed from midday to very late.

For full addresses, see Resources.

ARCHITOUR
A GUIDE TO MELBOURNE'S ICONIC BUILDINGS

In the past 20 years, Melbourne has undergone an architectural renaissance. New public arts buildings have flourished, while the standards of its residential and commercial developments are the highest in the country. And it is local architectural firms – Denton Corker Marshall, Wood Marsh, Fender Katsalidis Architects and the like – leading the charge. Much of their work within the city is ongoing and can be observed on a walking tour.

Many of the buildings that are featured here, including ACCA (Australian Centre for Contemporary Art, opposite), the Melbourne Museum (see p075) and Heide Museum of Modern Art (see p072), offer far more than just architectural splendour. Educational institutions are strongly represented too, but you might expect that in a city where one of the universities, RMIT, has an Innovation Professor of Architecture. If you visit the Centre for Ideas (see p078) at the Victorian College of the Arts, you should also check out the aptly dramatic design of the college's School of Drama (28 Dodd Street, T 9685 9225) by Edmond and Corrigan.

Some of the best examples of residential architecture in the city are Sean Godsell's 1997 Kew house (6 Hodgson Street) and two of Robin Boyd's houses: one in South Yarra (290 Walsh Street) and a crescent-shaped home in Brighton (2 Newbay Crescent). All three buildings are visible from the street.

For full addresses, see Resources.

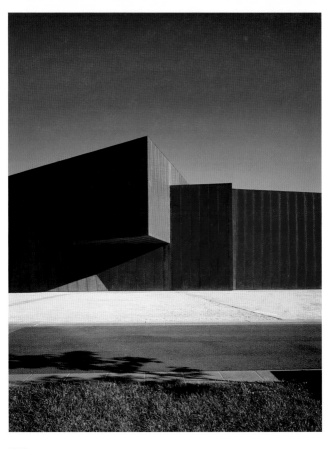

ACCA

Opened in 2002, the Australian Centre for Contemporary Art is a very urban building, yet resembles a large, rusting agricultural shed, like those seen in rural Australia. Set within a landscape of roads, train lines and warehouses, architects Roger Wood and Randall Marsh said they wanted to create 'a sculpture in which to show art'. The abstract steel exterior is in stark contrast to the glass foyer, which is accessed by the only obvious opening in the building, and the four white-walled gallery spaces of varying sizes. ACCA shows work by international and Australian contemporary artists, such as Barbara Kruger, Gillian Wearing and Callum Morton. *111 Sturt Street, T 9697 9999, www.accaonline.org.au*

Southern Cross Station
One of the busiest transport hubs in Australia was an uninspiring place to arrive in such a beautiful city until it was given a £280m makeover by UK-based architects Nicholas Grimshaw & Partners and locals Daryl Jackson Architects. The undulating roof acts as a filter to vent fumes naturally. Orange pods house the station administration.
Spencer Street/Collins Street

Newman College

Part of the University of Melbourne, Newman College was completed in 1918 and is the country's most significant structure designed by Walter Burley Griffin. Griffin worked for Frank Lloyd Wright and emigrated from Chicago in 1914 after winning a competition to design Canberra. This Catholic college, which was given a National Heritage listing in 2005, consists of a dining hall and two residential wings joined in strong geometric 'L' shapes, built in concrete with a sandstone veneer. The refectory dome, which is made of reinforced concrete, was one of the largest in Australia at the time of completion. The college is surrounded by park-like gardens, which were designed by Griffin's wife, Marion Mahoney.
887 Swanston Street, T 9347 5577, www.newman.unimelb.edu.au

QV

For this huge project – the rebuilding of an entire block – a raft of big-name firms were commissioned. On the site of the Queen Victoria Women's Hospital, which was designed by JJ Clark in 1911 and incorporated into the new layout, Denton Corker Marshall, John Wardle Architects, Kerstin Thompson Architects, Lyons Architects and McBride Charles Ryan have created a shopping mall, 600 apartments and the HQ of the mining company BHP Billiton. What is most interesting about the design, which was completed in 2004, is that one of the best-loved aspects of the city's grid – the laneways – has been amalgamated into the new layout.
Lonsdale Street/Swanston Street,
T 9658 0100, www.qv.com.au

Heide Museum of Modern Art
This complex in the suburb of Bulleen
consists of four buildings: the original
weatherboard farmhouse; Heide II, a
1965 modernist masterpiece by David
McGlashan; Heide III, a gallery space by
O'Connor + Houle, which opened in 2006
and houses a permanent art collection;
and the Sidney Myer Education Centre.
7 Templestowe Road, T 9850 1500,
www.heide.com.au

Monash City Council

One of just four buildings in Melbourne by Australia's best-known architect, the late Harry Seidler, this local government building in Glen Waverley sits on beautiful sloping parkland. The most outstanding aspect is the semi-circular skylight vault over a council chamber that otherwise has no windows. The building, completed in 1984, consists of two wings: one of two storeys containing the council chambers, mayor's office and function and meeting spaces; the other, three storeys housing the council offices. The two are linked by a high atrium foyer, which is used for public events, and a suspended bridge across the entry space.
293 Springvale Road, T 9518 3555,
www.monash.vic.gov.au

Melbourne Museum

When architects Denton Corker Marshall were commissioned to build the city's museum, they had to contend with its neighbour, the truly magnificent Royal Exhibition Building (Carlton Gardens). Designed by Joseph Reed in 1880 for the International Exhibition, and one of the only buildings of its kind left in the world, it was given a UNESCO World Heritage listing in 2004. Located on a slightly raised parkland site, Melbourne Museum, which opened in 2000, has all the elements of a DCM design: primary colours, tilted blocks, roof blades over the façade and boxes that house separate elements, such as the Aboriginal Centre, Bunjilaka.
11 Nicholson Street, T 8341 7777,
www.melbourne.museum.vic.gov.au

Webb Bridge

As much sculpture as pedestrian access, the Webb Bridge, a collaboration between Denton Corker Marshall, artist Robert Owen and engineers Arup, links Docklands with the east end of Southbank, across a 110m wide section of the Yarra River. Owen was inspired by the shape of an eel trap used by Aborigines who had once lived in the area, and the flow of the river. The final design is a series of hoops linked by a latticework of laser-cut steel. The steelwork was fabricated off site, then assembled on barges in Victoria Harbour and floated into position. The bridge was opened during a high tide in 2003.
Next to Charles Grimes Bridge Road

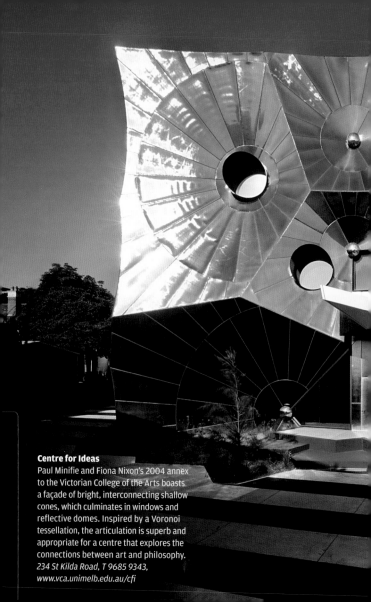

Centre for Ideas

Paul Minifie and Fiona Nixon's 2004 annex
to the Victorian College of the Arts boasts
a façade of bright, interconnecting shallow
cones, which culminates in windows and
reflective domes. Inspired by a Voronoi
tessellation, the articulation is superb and
appropriate for a centre that explores the
connections between art and philosophy.
234 St Kilda Road, T 9685 9343,
www.vca.unimelb.edu.au/cfi

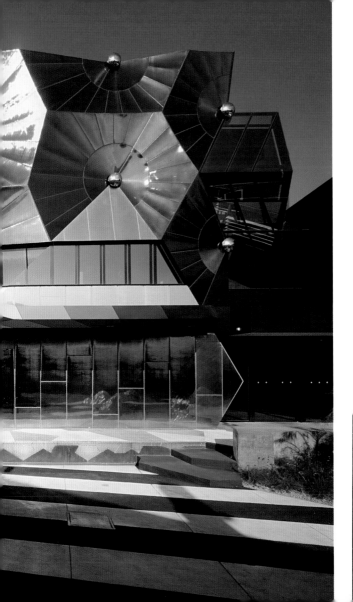

SHOPPING

THE BEST RETAIL THERAPY AND WHAT TO BUY

Melbourne has its share of soulless suburban mega-malls, but there are also areas that can make even the most dedicated shopaholic weep with joy. In an age of increasing homogeneity, Melbourne parades its individuality with pride. The city is blessed with good department stores – Myer (295 Lonsdale Street, T 9661 1111) and the upmarket David Jones (310 Bourke Street, T 9643 2222) – and quirky boutiques alike. In the Degraves Street Subway, also known as Campbell Arcade (enter at Flinders Street and Swanston Street), hunt out hidden gems, such as the excellent Corky Saint Clair (Shop 3, T 9663 5559) for tees, accessories and cards; Sticky (Shop 10, T 9654 8559) for 'zines and art books; and the Platform Artists Group gallery (www.platformartistsgroup.blogspot.com).

South Yarra is known for the upmarket stores of Toorak Road and Australian designer outlets such as Scanlan & Theodore (566 Chapel Street, T 9824 1800) and Alannah Hill (533 Chapel Street, T 9826 2755). Further along Chapel Street it's more offbeat: in Prahran, there's Fat at 272 (T 9510 2311), Gorman at 248 (T 9510 1151) and Chapel Street Bazaar at 217-223 (T 9529 1727).

Melbourne has its fair share of outdoor markets too; try Rose Street Artists Market (60 Rose Street, T 9419 5529) in Fitzroy on Saturdays and the Esplanade Market (Upper Esplanade, T 9534 0066), which sells mainly arts and crafts, in St Kilda on Sundays. *For full addresses, see Resources.*

Loco Lowriders

Forget sensible bikes that get you safely from A to B; Loco is all about looking good and attracting attention. This store has been selling imported low-rider bicycles, from the basic models to the Electra Rat Fink, for years. You can have your bike customised on site or take home a pile of accessories, such as a sissy bar or 14-inch twisted chrome handlebars, and do it yourself. If you like the look but haven't ridden a bike for years, there are T-shirts and videos so you can join the scene.
50 Brunswick Street, T 9416 4748, www.locolowriders.com

Hercynia Silva

Artist and carpenter Michael Conole and designer Viveka de Costa expanded their unique Clifton Hill store in March 2007 to display the work of Conole and another furniture-maker, Alex Stobie. The store also sells antique Japanese toys, 19th-century playpens, bogwood mourning jewellery, a carving of St Francis and anything else that is made, even partially, from wood. Conole and de Costa trawl auctions, markets and the internet to find their treasures. 'We're drawn to old and hard-to-find timbers and we're interested in folk objects,' says de Costa. To that end, Conole, a banjo player, has also started making and restoring that instrument. *656 Smith Street, T 9482 5770, www.hercyniasilva.com.au*

Order and Progress

Progress has been fast for this boutique, which focuses on South American labels. It began as an appointment-only showroom, opened a store at the end of 2005, then had to move into a larger space downstairs from its original home in Curtin House in early 2007. Look for pieces by Alexandre Herchovitch, Reinaldo Louren, Gloria Coelho and Neon, and accessories from all over the world, including Jack Gomme bags from Paris and Susan Bijl shoppers from the Netherlands. While you're in Curtin House, check out Someday (T 9654 6458) and Metropolis Bookshop (T 9663 2015), which are both on the same level.
Level 3, Curtin House,
252 Swanston Street, T 9654 1329,
www.orderandprogress.com.au

Alice Euphemia

The location of Karen Rieschieck's store in an arcade suits its quirky personality. The business started in 1997 but the idea is still the same: to bring small Australian and New Zealand clothing and accessories labels as well as exhibitions to the city. In stock for girls are Mad Cortes, former Karen Walker designer Mala Brajkovic, and hand-stitched one-offs by Who is Dead Martin?. Boys are offered Romance Was Born, Beat Poët and Josh Goot. Be sure to seek out the Iggy and Lou Lou porcelain jewellery and the house brand One Trick Pony, which is created in conjunction with artists and industrial designers.
Shop 6, Cathedral Arcade,
37 Swanston Street, T 9650 4300,
www.aliceeuphemia.com

Pieces of Eight

Melbourne is renowned for the standard of its contemporary jewellery-making and this gallery in North Fitzroy is a showcase for the city's emerging talent. Most of the designers represented are Australian art school graduates (non-jewellery pieces are often displayed too) and their work, in anything from precious metals to more humble materials, is either one-off or limited edition, so you're guaranteed to stand out from the fashion crowd. There is an on-site workshop as well, and many of the designers work to commission. *635 Brunswick Street, T 9497 8121, www.piecesofeight.com.au*

Assin

The Pinto family – mother Francelina and sisters Fernanda and Lucy – are well known in Melbourne for their fashion-forward boutiques, including their latest, Assin. The architectural interior sits in a minimalist concrete bunker and the stunning setting and designer clothes combine to produce a reverent ambience. Classic pieces by Hussein Chalayan, Viktor & Rolf, Dior Homme, Marni and Dirk Schönberger arrive straight from the runways of Europe and are hung beside outstanding Australian designers such as Akira. Not to be outdone, the Pintos also have their own label, Assin, as well as a tightly edited selection of accessories for both men and women. If you have time, check out the Pintos' South Yarra store, Assin Outlet (T 9827 4665), as well.
138 Little Collins Street, T 9654 0158, www.assin.com.au

SPORTS AND SPAS
WORK OUT, CHILL OUT OR JUST WATCH

Melburnians take their sport seriously. Australian Football (also called Aussie Rules or AFL) was born here and is the city's main religion. Everyone has a team and barracks for them with fervour during the winter. Even if you have no idea what's going on, it's worth watching a game for the spectacle (visit www.afl.com.au for details). The summer sport, cricket, is also revered – if you want to watch a match at the MCG (see p012), make sure you buy tickets well in advance. Other big drawcards are the Melbourne Cup, held during the Spring Racing carnival, the Australian Grand Prix and the Australian Open tennis tournament.

If you want to keep in shape, the city's historic Melbourne City Baths (420 Swanston Street, T 9663 5888) and Carlton Baths (see p092) cater for a total fitness experience, while the nationwide chain Fitness First (www.fitnessfirst.com.au) offers a two-week membership that can be purchased online. For those who prefer pampering to perspiration, the luxurious Chuan Spa (see p090) at the Langham Hotel and Aurora Spa Retreat (2 Acland Street, T 9536 1130) at The Prince (see p020) are highly recommended. If you're after fresh air but don't fancy anything too strenuous, lawn bowls is enjoying a renaissance. Try Brekky Bowls at the Fitzroy Victoria Bowling & Sports Club (Edinburgh Gardens, 578 Brunswick Street, T 9481 3137) on Sundays from 11am.

For full addresses, see Resources.

South Pacific Health Club

Housed in an historic building, this huge health club has state-of-the-art facilities and includes the famous St Kilda Sea Baths (above). Here, you'll find a heated 25m indoor seawater pool, hydrotherapy spa pool and steam rooms. Within the same building, Li'Tya Spa Dreaming (T 9525 3288) incorporates Aboriginal techniques and ingredients into its treatments. Book a Kodo Rocks stone massage therapy in a room overlooking the ocean. This complex is just the ticket for a workout followed by a relaxing spa session.
10-18 Jacka Boulevard, T 9525 4888, www.southpacifichc.com.au

Chuan Spa

Located in the Langham Hotel, Chuan has become the relaxation destination of choice for stressed-out city folk. Enter its beautiful, softly lit rooms, decorated in dark woods and cream, and you will instantly feel calmer. There's an emphasis on merging traditional Chinese therapies with practices better known to Westerners, such as facials and body scrubs. The 90-minute Chuan Stone Therapy, a massage utilising smooth hot and cold stones, will leave you feeling as if you're floating on clouds. Allow time after your treatment to enjoy the excellent facilities, which include a steam room and sauna, and also to lie by the pool, which overlooks the city. *1 Southgate Avenue, T 8696 8111, www.chuanspa.com*

Carlton Baths

The first pool was built on this site in the early 1900s, and although some heritage elements have been retained in ongoing upgrades, the latest incarnation, by the architect Peter Elliot, includes a lot more than just a swimming spot. The outdoor 25m pool, surrounded by green lawns, is in use from 1 October to 30 April, while the health club, spa and sauna are open year-round. There's a good timetable of fitness classes and as the centre is run by the YMCA, the prices are reasonable too. *248 Rathdowne Street, T 9347 3677, www.carltonbaths.ymca.org.au*

Breathe

This yoga and Pilates studio in a sleek, light-filled, 140-year-old former jeweller's warehouse is a paradise for those who like their exercise *sans* treadmill. There are 65 classes per week, suitable for all levels of fitness. Especially good for curing jetlag is the 'Sleep' class, which will recharge your body and soul.
289 Little Collins Street, T 9662 1500,
www.breathewellbeing.com.au

ESCAPES

WHERE TO GO IF YOU WANT TO LEAVE TOWN

As if this city didn't appear to have it all, it is possible to head in almost any direction from Melbourne and find lively country towns, wine-growing regions, beaches and staggeringly beautiful coastline. And if you need additional getaway inspiration, it's always worth asking a local where they go for a short break.

One of the most popular trips out of town is a drive along the Great Ocean Road that stretches all the way to Adelaide in South Australia. It follows the Shipwreck Coast (and it's called that for good reason) and passes the famous Bells Beach, the fashionable resort town of Lorne and the quiet fishing village of Apollo Bay. If you're a surfer, you'll love this drive, although there is a distinct lack of luxury accommodation along the way.

Even closer are the resort towns of the Mornington Peninsula, including Sorrento and Portsea (see p098). Here, swimming and surfing are among the most popular pastimes, although you can go on dolphin-watching cruises and sailing expeditions too.

Those who prefer dry land should head for the wineries of the Yarra Valley. The main town, Healesville, is 45 minutes to the east, and there are more than 30 wine producers in the area. One of the best is Yering Station (38 Melba Highway, Yarra Glen, T 03 9730 0100), which, apart from making superb wines, has an excellent tasting area, a restaurant, a produce store and a small art gallery. *For full addresses, see Resources.*

Lake House, Daylesford

Once at the centre of Victoria's gold rush, Daylesford, about 80 minutes' drive from Melbourne, is better known today as a spa town. The stylish and relaxing Lake House has 33 rooms and suites set alongside the Salus Spa, which features treatment rooms in private treehouses and its own bottled water. Lake House is also rightly famous for its restaurant, where chef Alla Wolf-Tasker has been creating dishes of such excellence that this is regarded as one of the best eateries in the country. You'll also find great golf courses and a lively arts scene in the area.

King Street, T 03 5348 3329,
www.lakehouse.com.au

Zealandia, Portsea

This classic 1950s beach house has been restored right down to its blue mosaic swimming pool and original furniture. Huge windows look out over tranquil gardens, there's a massive entertaining deck under the cantilevered roof, an open fireplace and modern kitchen and bathroom facilities. Located in Portsea, a seaside resort on the Mornington Peninsula, Zealandia is about two hours' drive from the city. Favoured by wealthy Melburnians, it has three large bedrooms plus sleeping space in the second living area, making it a perfect destination for a group. It's all about unwinding here — you can walk to either of the two beaches, hire a yacht from Portsea Yacht Charters (T 04 1701 2976) and have a sunset dinner overlooking the sea from the bistro at Portsea Hotel (T 03 5984 2213).

T 03 9650 2523, www.zealandia.com.au

Shadowfax Winery, Werribee Park

Just 20 minutes' drive from the centre of the city is this dusty, historic park, which boasts more attractions than you can cram into a weekend. Stay at the Sofitel Mansion & Spa (T 03 9731 4000), where architects Wood Marsh added an award-winning spa wing to a heritage-listed building. In the grounds is the Shadowfax Winery, also designed by Wood Marsh, which, with its rusted sheet-metal panels and terracotta interior, has been built to blend in with the natural surroundings. The winery itself is state of the art and produces a range of fine wines, available for tasting. Also in Werribee Park are the historic Chirnside Mansion, a sculpture walk, the State Rose Garden and the Open Range Zoo, a small-scale safari park.
K Road, Werribee, T 03 9731 4420,
www.shadowfax.com.au

Boyd Baker House, Bacchus Marsh

In isolated bushland 45 minutes' drive west of Melbourne is one of Australia's most important modernist houses, which since 2007 has been available to rent. Designed by Robin Boyd, considered to be one of Australia's leading architects and social commentators, the five-bedroom Baker House was completed in 1966. Arranged around a central courtyard, the house features curved internal walls made out of locally hewn sandstone. The glass walls of the outer rooms give the feeling of actually living in the bush. The smaller Dower House, also by Robin Boyd, and a library designed by Sir Roy Grounds in 1979, are part of the complex.
Long Forest Conservation Reserve, T 03 8508 6444, www.bakerhouse.com.au

Boyd Baker House, Bacchus Marsh

NOTES

SKETCHES AND MEMOS

RESOURCES
CITY GUIDE DIRECTORY

A

ACCA 065
111 Sturt Street
T 9697 9999
www.accaonline.org.au

Alannah Hill 080
533 Chapel Street
T 9826 2755
www.alannahhill.com.au

Alice Euphemia 084
Shop 6, Cathedral Arcade
37 Swanston Street
T 9650 4300
www.aliceeuphemia.com

Amor y Locura 034
77 Gertrude Street
T 9486 0270
www.amorylocura.com

Anna Schwartz Gallery 036
185 Flinders Lane
T 9654 6131
www.annaschwartzgallery.com

Assin 086
138 Little Collins Street
T 9654 0158
www.assin.com.au

Assin Outlet 086
Shop 3, 177 Toorak Road
T 9827 4665
www.assin.com.au

Aurora Spa Retreat 088
The Prince
2 Acland Street
T 9536 1130
www.aurorasparetreat.com

B

Il Bacaro 062
168-170 Little Collins Street
T 9654 6778
www.ilbacaro.com.au

Bar Lourinhã 062
37 Little Collins Street
T 9663 7890
www.barlourinha.com.au

Bistro Vue 042
Entrance via New Chancery laneway
430 Little Collins Street
T 9691 3838
www.vuedemonde.com.au

Bobby's Cuts 036
Shop 4
237-239 Flinders Lane/Scott Alley
T 9663 4030
www.myspace.com/bobbyscuts

Books for Cooks 034
233-235 Gertrude Street
T 8415 1415
www.booksforcooks.com.au

Botanical 023
169 Domain Road
T 9820 7888
www.thebotanical.com.au

Boyd Baker House 101
Robin Boyd Baker Compound
Long Forest Conservation Reserve
Bacchus Marsh
T 03 8508 6444
www.bakerhouse.com.au

Breathe 094
289 Little Collins Street
T 9662 1500
www.breathewellbeing.com.au

HOTELS

ADDRESSES AND ROOM RATES

Adelphi 022
  Room rates:
  double, A$220-A$320
  187 Flinders Lane
  T 9650 7555
  www.adelphi.com.au

The Como 017
  Room rates:
  double, from A$600;
  Spa Suite, from A$640;
  Open-Plan Suite, from A$640
  630 Chapel Street
  T 9825 2222
  www.mirvachotels.com

Crown Towers 030
  Room rates:
  double, A$285-A$350;
  Deluxe Suite, A$500-A$640;
  Crystal Club Villa, A$1,250
  8 Whiteman Street
  T 9292 6868
  www.crowntowers.com.au

The Hatton 023
  Room rates:
  double, A$195;
  Superior Room, A$220;
  Eastern Balcony Suite, A$300
  65 Park Street
  T 9868 4800
  www.hatton.com.au

Hotel Lindrum 028
  Room rates:
  double, A$240;
  Deluxe Room, A$460;
  Junior Suite, A$500
  26 Flinders Street
  T 9668 1111
  www.hotellindrum.com.au

The Lyall Hotel 016
  Room rates:
  double, A$320-A$500;
  Suite 401, A$900
  14 Murphy Street
  T 9868 8222
  www.thelyall.com

The Marque Hotel 026
  Room rates:
  double, A$150;
  Executive Room, A$205;
  Play Room, A$220
  35-37 Fitzroy Street
  T 8530 8888
  www.rendezvoushotels.com

Park Hyatt 016
  Room rates:
  double, A$315
  1 Parliament Square
  Off Parliament Place
  T 9224 1234
  www.melbourne.park.hyatt.com

The Prince 020
  Room rates:
  double, A$305;
  Room 413, A$630
  2 Acland Street
  T 9536 1111
  www.theprince.com.au

Sofitel 016
  Room rates:
  double, A$210-A$525
  25 Collins Street
  T 9653 0000
  www.sofitelmelbourne.com.au

WALLPAPER* CITY GUIDES

Editorial Director
Richard Cook

Art Director
Loran Stosskopf
City Editor
Carrie Hutchinson
Editor
Rachael Moloney
Executive
Managing Editor
Jessica Firmin
Travel Bookings Editor
Sara Henrichs

Chief Designer
Benjamin Blossom
Designer
Daniel Shrimpton

Map Illustrator
Russell Bell

Photography Editor
Christopher Lands
Photography Assistant
Robin Key

Chief Sub-Editor
Jeremy Case
Sub-Editor
Vicky McGinlay
Assistant Sub-Editor
Milly Nolan

Intern
Jemima Hills

Wallpaper* Group
Editor-in-Chief
Tony Chambers
Publishing Director
Andrew Black
Publisher
Neil Sumner

Contributors
Meirion Pritchard
Ellie Stathaki

Wallpaper* ® is a
registered trademark
of IPC Media Limited

All prices are correct at
time of going to press,
but are subject to change.

PHAIDON

Phaidon Press Limited
Regent's Wharf
All Saints Street
London N1 9PA

Phaidon Press Inc
180 Varick Street
New York, NY 10014

Phaidon® is a registered
trademark of Phaidon
Press Limited

www.phaidon.com

First published 2007
© 2007 IPC Media Limited

ISBN 978 0 7148 4746 7

A CIP Catalogue record for
this book is available from
the British Library.

Printed in China

PHOTOGRAPHERS

Markus Bachmann
The Prince, pp020-021
The Hatton, p023,
pp024-025
Hotel Lindrum, pp028-029
Southern Cross Station,
pp068-069

Peter Bennets
New Gold Mountain,
p050, p051

Wolfram Janzer/Artur
Federation Square,
pp014-015
Interior, ACCA, pp066-067

Daniel Mahon
Barrie Barton, p063

Trevor Mein
MCG, p012

Derek Swalwell
Melbourne city view,
inside front cover
Melbourne Gateway,
pp010-011
Republic Tower, p013
The Como, p017,
pp018-019
The Marque Hotel, p027
Mario's, p033
Tongue and Groove, p034
The Gertrude Street
Enoteca, p035

Taxi Dining Room, p038
The Croft Institute, p039
Cookie, p041
MoVida, p044
Pearl Restaurant + Bar,
p045
Piadina Slow Food, p046
Melbourne Wine Room,
p047
Madame Brussels,
pp052-053
Ffour, p054
Polly, p058
ACCA, p065
Newman College, p070
QV, p071
Heide Museum of Modern
Art, pp072-073
Monash City Council, p074
Melbourne Museum, p075
Centre for Ideas,
pp078-079
Loco Lowriders, p081
Hercynia Silva, p082
Order and Progress, p083
Alice Euphemia, p084
Pieces of Eight, p085
Assin, pp086-087
South Pacific Health Club,
p089
Carlton Baths, pp092-093
Breathe, pp094-095

MELBOURNE
A COLOUR-CODED GUIDE TO THE HOT 'HOODS

CENTRAL BUSINESS DISTRICT
The CBD is lively both day and night as it's packed with shops, restaurants and bars

SOUTHBANK
An entertainment complex, five-star hotels and the city's Arts Centre overlook the Yarra

CARLTON
The city's authentic Italian quarter is full of superb trattorias and cafés, as you'd expect

ST KILDA
This bayside suburb with bookstores, bars and cafés runs down to the waterfront and pier

SOUTH YARRA
High-end boutiques, top eateries and plenty of green space give this district a village feel

FITZROY
This arty, up-and-coming, bohemian enclave is home to Melbourne's Spanish community

For a full description of each neighbourhood, see the Introduction.
Featured venues are colour-coded, according to the district in which they are located.